The best recipes from Brittany

We should like to thank Faïenceries de Quimper H.B. Henriot
who supplied the hand-painted platters and plates
on which the dishes were presented.

Recipes by Ray̶n̶u̶

Photographs by Claude Herlédan

Translated by Angela Moyon

Some of the dishes photographed were made by catering students
at the Paraclet Private High School in Quimper
under the direction of Mr. Begel, their teacher,
and Mr. Sergeaut, their project leader.

Éditions
OUEST-FRANCE

introduction

The earliest inhabitants of the Breton coastal area were known as the «shellfish eaters». In those days, the cold climate and marshes made the hinterland inaccessible and food consisted mainly of seafood. Gradually, as the climate improved, the local diet began to include game, roots, and wild berries. In modern times, thanks to the use of fertilisation, people can enjoy fresh fruit and vegetables in abundance in Brittany. The moors have slowly given way to lush, green pasture on which cows graze, producing milk that is turned into butter of a quality unrivalled elsewhere, flavoured with grains of sea salt. This is just one example of how closely linked maritime and rural traditions have remained through the ages. Here, then, are a few recipes from a region in which food tastes as it should, thanks to a style of cooking that is as unpretentious as it is flavoursome.

Seafood
Platter

Per person

*4 European or
Japanese oysters,
3 clams,
6 butter clams,
1 small handful of
winkles,
3 scampi,
1/2 crab
or spider-crab,
mayonnaise,
shallot-flavoured
vinegar,
lemon,
salted butter,
rye bread*

Preparation
Put the unopened oysters and clams in the bottom of the refrigerator or in a cool place, covered with a damp cloth.

Winkles
Rinse well under running water. Place in a saucepan, cover with cold water and add a heaped dsp. of sea salt per litre of water. Place over a medium heat and bring to boil. Remove from heat, leave to stand for 2 mins, and drain.

Scampi
Place live in a large saucepan of boiling water containing salt and vinegar (1 tsp. vinegar per 2 litres water). Stir and bring back to the boil. If the scampi are small, drain immediately. For larger scampi, leave to stand for 2 mins. before draining.
Serve warm. If necessary, they can be put back into boiling water for a few seconds just before making up the seafood platter.
Golden Rule: Never cook more than 1 kilo of scampi at any one time. It takes too long to bring the water back to the boil and the scampi loses its crisp texture.

Crabs or spider-crabs
Wash under running water, brush if necessary, then place live in a large pan of heavily-salted boiling water (preferably sea water) containing vinegar (1 dsp. vinegar per 2 litres water). Boil for 15 mins. (medium-sized crabs) or 25 mins. (larger crabs). Drain, tilting the crabs forward so that any water that has entered the shell can run out.
To serve: When they have cooled slightly (but while they are still warm), break the claws and nippers off from the shell. Break large nippers with a wooden mallet or a hammer - do not attempt to peel. Remove the contents of the shell by pushing a strong knife blade in beside the head and levering off. Throw away the gills attached to each side of the body. Cut the body into quarters and serve warm.
Oysters, clams, butter clams: Open immediately before serving.
The platter: Lay a bed of seaweed on a large platter and lay out the shellfish and seafood. Serve with mayonnaise, shallot-flavoured vinegar and lemon.

Seafood Platter.

«Palais»-
Style
Scallops

Serves 4.
Preparation: 20 mins.
Cooking: 15 mins.

3 to 4 large scallops with coral per person,
1/2 tsp. pink garlic (finely crushed),
2 medium-sized shallots (finely chopped),
4 generous dsp. crème fraîche,
125 g salted butter,
salt, pepper

Open scallops while fresh. Remove flesh and wash under running water. Remove and discard beard and the black gut.

Separate flesh and coral. Thinly slice flesh and place flesh and coral in a sieve.

Set aside 4 to 8 empty scallop shells.

Melt a knob (50 g) of butter in a large pan. Gently cook shallots over a low heat for 2 to 3 mins. without allowing to brown.

Add scallops and garlic and cook gently for 2 mins. stirring all the time (scallops should remain translucent). Season with salt and pepper then remove from pan with a strainer spoon and set aside.

Add crème fraîche to stock in pan. Reduce over a high heat until thick and creamy (approx. 6 mins). Add a knob of butter and scallops then remove from heat.

Fill empty shells with scallops in cream sauce and top with a small knob of butter. Place in preheated oven (Th. 6 or 200° C) for 15 mins. until lightly browned.

5

Riec-Style Mussels

Serves 6.
Preparation and cooking:
20 minutes

40 cl Muscadet,
6 chopped shallots,
3 cloves garlic (chopped),
1 apple (e.g. Cox's) peeled and diced,
6 dsp. chopped parsley,
3 dsp. breadcrumbs,
100 g salted butter,
pepper

2.5 kg washed, scraped mussels,

Lightly fry the shallots, garlic and apple in the butter in a large pan over a medium heat for 3 to 4 minutes, stirring continuously.

Add the parsley and breadcrumbs, stir to mix, then pour in the white wine. Cook for 5 minutes over a high heat until the liquid has reduced by half.

Throw in the mussels, season with pepper, and cover. Shake pan to ensure that the mussels are well-coated.

Leave to cook, stirring occasionally, until the mussels have all opened.

Pour into a large bowl and serve.

Riec-Style Mussels.

Stuffed Butter Clams

Serves 4.
Preparation: 35 minutes.
Cooking: 10 minutes under grill

1 kg butter clams,
150 g salted butter,
2 shallots (chopped),
2 cloves garlic (chopped),
1 small onion (chopped),
1 large pinch curry powder,
6 dsp. chopped parsley and chives,
3 slices French toast or 1 large slice bread,
salt, pepper,
breadcrumbs

Cook the clams in their own juice in a covered pan over a high heat, shaking the pan frequently.

Remove from heat as soon as the shellfish begin to open. Take off the top shells and place bottom shell, with flesh, on a baking tray. Set aside 15 cl of the cooking liquor.

Preparing the stuffing: Soak the French toast or bread in the clam cooking liquor and mix thoroughly. Heat the butter in a pan over a medium heat and cook the shallot-garlic-onion mixture for 3 minutes, stirring continuously. Add the chopped parsley and chives, curry powder, pepper, and the French toast mixture dampened with the cooking liquor. Simmer for 5 to 8 minutes. Taste and add salt if required. Pour one spoonful of stuffing onto each clam. Sprinkle lightly with breadcrumbs and grill for 10 minutes (or bake for 20 minutes in oven preheated to Th. 7, 210 °C).

The same recipe can be used for shiny or other species of clams and mussels.

Stuffed Butter Clams.

Angèle's Seafood Gratin

Serves 4.
Preparation: 35 mins.
Cooking: 20 mins.

1 kg fresh mussels (washed and scraped),
8 scallops with their coral,
12 cooked shrimps (large, peeled),
1 small jar lobster butter,
1 large shallot (finely chopped),
1/2 glass vinegar,
100 g salted butter,
1 tsp. tomato puree (or ketchup),
1/2 tsp. curry powder,
4 dsp. cider brandy,
4 dsp. thick crème fraîche,
1 level dsp. flour,
3 dsp. breadcrumbs,
salt, pepper.

Open the mussels by placing them in a saucepan over a high heat and shaking frequently. When they can be easily detached, remove from shells and place in a basin (keep back one bowl of mussel stock).

Add remainder of seafood. Cook shallots in vinegar in a saucepan (taking care not to overcook) until liquid reduces to one dsp.

Add flour mixed with a small quantity of mussel stock, followed by tomato puree, curry powder and brandy.

Cook for 2 mins, stirring continuously. Remove from heat, beat in crème fraîche and add butter in small knobs.

Blend then season with salt and pepper. Finally, add lobster butter. Grease a gratin dish and pour in seafood.

Cover with sauce. Sprinkle with breadcrumbs and bake for 20 mins. in a preheated oven (Th. 6 or 200° C) until golden brown.

Lobster à l'**armoricaine**

Serves 4.
Preparation: 45 minutes.
Cooking: 20 minutes.

2 live lobster
(750 - 800 g each),
2 chopped shallots,
1 large clove garlic
(crushed),
3 tomatoes
(peeled and
seeded)
or 1/2 tin
peeled
tomatoes,
1 small bouquet garni
(thyme, bay,
parsley),
1 sprig tarragon,
1 pinch dried red
«porphyra» seaweed,
1 piece dried penny
bun,

35 cl Muscadet-sur-
lie,
2 dsp. cognac,
1/2 tsp. curry
powder,
1/3 tsp. cayenne
pepper,
1/2 tsp. sugar,
10 cl olive oil, salt,
pepper

To cut lobster

Lay the lobster on a working surface and hold with the left hand, keeping the claws to the right. Split the body open with a strong, short-bladed knife, working from left to right. Turn the lobster round and split the tail. Remove the intestine (grey gut underneath the pink flesh in tail) and throw away. Remove and discard the sand sac.

Set aside in a bowl the creamy greenish-coloured matter and the liquid contained in body. Cut the claws off at the body joint and break open the nippers with the handle of the knife. Slice the half-tails in two along the joints.

Preparation

As soon as the lobster have been cut open:

Pour the olive oil into a high-sided frying pan and warm over a high heat until it almost begins to smoke. Place the pieces of lobster in the pan. Move around with a spatula to ensure that the flesh is evenly cooked and the shell turns red.

Pour in the cognac and set alight.

Turn down to a medium heat, add the shallots and garlic, stir for a few seconds, then add the chopped tomatoes, crumbled dried penny bun, pinch of «porphyra» seaweed, sugar, bouquet garni, tarragon, curry powder, Cayenne pepper, salt and pepper.

Simmer for 5 minutes, stirring to ensure that the lobster takes in the flavours of the various herbs and spices. Pour in the white wine, cover and cook for 20 minutes

Remove the lobster from the pan and set aside in a basin covered with aluminium foil so that it does not dry out.

Pour the creamy matter and the liquid taken from the body of the lobster into the pan.

Reduce the sauce for 5 minutes over a high heat then remove the tarragon and bouquet garni. Whisk the sauce in a blender.

Pour the sauce back into the pan, add the pieces of lobster, and simmer for 10 minutes over a gentle heat.

To serve

Lay out the pieces of lobster on a serving dish and pour the sauce over the top. Serve with creole rice. Remember to provide finger-wipes.

This recipe for lobster can be made several hours in advance and reheated at the last minute.

Also suitable for freezing.

Mélanie's
Lobster in
Cream Sauce

Serves 4.
Preparation: 30 mins.
Cooking: 30 mins.

2 lobsters
(*800 g* each),
3 dsp. olive oil,
100 g butter,

6 medium shallots
(*80 g*, chopped),
4 large dsp. of thick
crème fraîche
(*200 g*),
1 large glass (*20 cl*)
of Muscadet,
2 – 3 dsp. good
cognac,
1 dsp. veal stock
granules,
1 heaped dsp.
cornflour,
1 dsp. butter,
salt, pepper,
cayenne pepper

Split the lobster while still alive. To do so, push a thick-bladed knife into the base of the head. This will kill the lobster immediately and it will not suffer. Cut body into four pieces, remove legs and claws and break with knife handle.

Cut head in two, remove greenish creamy substance (the coral) and the transparent liquid and set aside in a bowl. Discard the sand sac which is also in the head.

Gently cook chopped shallots in a small saucepan with 100 g butter over a very low heat until transparent (10 mins).

Heat olive oil in a pan over a high heat and when it is very hot add pieces of lobster. Cook quickly on all sides, moving around pan until shells are bright red. Pour in cognac and flambé.

Sprinkle on cayenne pepper, salt and pepper then add shallots, wine and veal stock, and stir. Bring back to the boil.

Reduce heat, cover and simmer for 30 mins. stirring occasionally. Remove pieces of lobster with a strainer spoon, lay out on a serving dish, and keep warm over a low heat.

Filter stock from pan, return to heat and reduce slightly. Bind sauce with the spoonful of softened butter, cornflour and the coral set aside in a bowl.

Stir until thick without allowing to boil.

Add cream and rectify seasoning.

Pour sauce over lobster and serve immediately with rice.

Lobster à l'armoricaine.

Bass in Salt.

Bass
in **Salt**

Serves 6.
Preparation: 5 minutes.
Cooking: 40 minutes.

1 bass (approx.
1,5 kg gutted but
with scales left on),
1,5 kg grey sea salt,
3 dsp.
algae-flavoured
court-bouillon,
pepper,
1 large handful fresh
seaweed (optional)

Preheat the oven to Th.8 or 250 ° C.
Carefully wash the interior to remove any traces of blood then season with pepper.
Lay a large piece of aluminium foil on a baking dish.
Blend the grey sea salt with the court-bouillon and spread 1/3 of the mixture over the foil. Lay the fish on the foil and cover with the remainder of the salt mixture, pressing it well around the fish with your fingers.
Bake for 40 minutes in the oven.

Lay seaweed around a large serving dish and slip the bass into the centre. Show it to the guests before breaking the salt casing and removing the salt along with the scales and skin.
Divide the fish into fillets, lay on a hot dish and serve with white butter sauce and boiled potatoes.

Belon
Fish Stew

Serves 8.
Preparation: 1 hour.
Cooking: 25 minutes.

600 g conger eel (from near head) cut into thick slices,
1 garfish,
1 wrasse,
1 sea bream
(approx. 1 kg),
3 red gurnet,
4 medium-sized mackerel,
4 whiting,
3 large whiting-pout,
4 sliced onions,
1.5 kg peeled, quartered potatoes,
1 bouquet garni (thyme, bay, parsley),
100 g salt fat (or salted butter), salt, pepper

Clean and gut the fish, remove the scales, cut off the heads and set aside. Keep the various species of fish separate.

Preparation of stock

Place the fish heads and bouquet garni in a saucepan. Add 3 litres water and boil for 30 minutes

Filter the stock and set aside.

Preparation of fish stew

Heat the salt fat (or butter) in a large pan over a medium heat. Fry the sliced onions for 3 minutes until pale golden in colour then add the potatoes and cook until light brown, stirring continuously (N.B. ensure onions do not burn as this gives the stew a bitter taste).

Pour in the stock, add the conger eel, and season with salt. Add 1 tsp. pepper.

Bring to the boil over a high heat then lower the heat and boil for 15 minutes

Add the firmer fish (garfish, mackerel, wrasse, and sea bream). Simmer for 5 minutes without covering the pan.

Finally, add the softer fish (whiting, whiting-pout, red gurnet).

Simmer for a further 5 minutes.

Cover, remove from the heat, and leave to stand for 5 minutes to allow the fish to cook through.

To serve

Carefully remove the fish with a slice and lay out on one or two serving dishes. Surround with potatoes.

Keep the stock warm on a low heat. It is served last (after the fish).

Serve the fish stew with a good herb-flavoured vinaigrette dressing (parsley, chervil, chives or even tarragon).

Then serve the stock in soup bowls, over slices of stale bread.

Nantes-Style
White Butter
Sauce

Serves 6.
Preparation: 20 minutes.

5 - 6 grey shallots,
30 cl good Muscadet-sur-lie,
300 g salted butter,
1 heaped dsp. fresh double cream,
salt, white pepper

Cut the butter into pieces on a plate and set aside at warm room temperature.

Peel and finely chop the shallots. Place in a saucepan with the white wine and reduce over a low heat to the equivalent of approx. 2 spoonfuls.

Remove from the heat and gradually add the butter, whipping the sauce until it resembles a smooth cream.

Season with salt and pepper. Add the fresh cream, and pour into a slightly-warmed sauce boat.

If the sauce is not to be served immediately, keep warm in a tepid bain-marie, whisking occasionally.

Buccaneer's Stew

Serves 6.
Preparation: 90 minutes.
Cooking: 15 minutes
+ 5 minutes to reheat.

1 carrot (peeled and washed),
1 small stick celery,
2 onions (peeled),
1 clove garlic,
1 bouquet garni (thyme, bay, parsley),
1/2 bottle Muscadet,
1 dose saffron,
1 dsp. coriander seeds,
100 g salted butter,
salt, pepper

For mayonnaise
1 egg yolk,
1 tsp. mustard,
20 cl oil,
1 tsp. vinegar,
1 large clove garlic (crushed),
salt, pepper

2 red gurnet,
1 garfish,
6 slices hake (or pollack),
1 small wrasse,
3 whiting,
1 kg mussels (scraped and washed),
1 spider crab (approx. 1 kg),
1.2 kg potatoes,
1 leek (peeled and washed),

Prepare the fish - remove the scales, gut, cut off the heads and fins, and divide into portions. Set the fish heads to one side.

Cook the mussels over a high heat in a covered pan, shaking frequently. As soon as the mussels are open and come away easily from their shells, remove from the heat and take out of the shells. Filter the liquor and set aside.

Preparation of stock

Pour the Muscadet into the pan. Add 3/4 litre water, the mussel liquor, fish heads, leek, carrot, celery, bouquet garni, clove of garlic (with skin), coriander seeds, salt and pepper (N.B. remember that the mussel liquor is already salted).

Bring to the boil over a high heat. Wash and brush the spider crab then place in the stock. Cook for 15 minutes Remove the crab, filter the stock and set aside.

Preparation of stew

Chop the onions. Peel the potatoes and cut into thick slices. Heat 100 g salted butter in a pan and cook the onions for 2 minutes until golden. Add the potatoes and cook until golden, for 5 minutes, stirring continuously. Add the saffron and stock.

Bring to the boil over a high heat then lower the heat and cook for 15 minutes.

Lay the fish over the potatoes. Reheat until simmering, remove from the heat and cover the pan.

Remove the meat from the body and nippers of the crab. Set some of the white meat aside. Keep separate the liver and the yellow, creamy flesh.

Make a mayonnaise with the egg yolk, mustard, salt, pepper, and oil. Add the vinegar last, with the crushed garlic, liver and creamy flesh from crab.

To serve

Reheat the stew, simmering for 3 minutes Add the white crab meat and mussels.

Serve from the pan.

Use soup plates. Accompany with the mayonnaise served in a sauce boat.

It is the hostess who serves each guest, putting pieces of fish, potatoes and a ladleful of stock in each plate.

Buccaneer's Stew.

« Marie Cigogne »
Fillets
of **sole**

Serves 6.
Preparation: 20 mins.
Cooking: 20 mins.
+ 15 mins.

6 large fillets of sole,
1 orange,
1 medium glass
(15 cl) dry white
wine,
3 dsp. port,
1 sprig thyme +
1 bay leaf,

1 tsp. coriander seeds,
1 small jar lobster
butter,
1 pinch curry powder,
2 dsp. thick crème
fraîche,
salt, pepper,
6 small mushrooms
(as fresh as possible
and very white),
2 carrots (grated)
+ 1 small cucumber
(grated),
1 onion (finely
chopped) +
1 leek (white part
only, finely chopped),
2 dsp. chervil
(chopped).

Grate 1 tsp. of orange zest then squeeze juice. Mix juice and zest in a saucepan with wine, port, thyme, bay leaf and coriander. Reduce by one-half over a gentle heat.

Sieve and blend in lobster butter, curry and crème fraîche. Season with salt and pepper. Pour into an ovenproof dish, add grated or chopped vegetables and sliced mushrooms. Cook for 20 mins. in preheated oven (Th. 6 or 200° C).

Reduce temperature to Th. 5 or 170° C and add fillets of sole (folded in half) to dish of vegetables. Cook for a further 15 to 18 mins.

Remove from oven and sprinkle with chervil.

Serve with fresh pasta.

Chicken
in
Fouesnant
Cider

Serves 4.
Preparation: 15 minutes.
Cooking: 45 minutes.

1 large chicken
(1.2 kg),
30 cl dry cider,
4 dsp. cider brandy,
6 thinly-sliced shallots,
4 dsp. double cream,
2 apples (e.g. Cox's),
100 g salted butter,
salt, pepper

Lightly brown the chicken over a medium heat in a large pan with half the butter. Add the shallots and fry for 3 to 4 minutes until golden.

Pour in the brandy and cider, season with salt and pepper, cover, and turn down the heat. Simmer for 20 minutes.

Add the peeled apples cut into quarters and the remainder of the butter. Cook for 5 minutes in an uncovered pan over a high heat until the sauce has reduced.

Add the fresh cream, cover, and cook for a further 20 minutes over a low heat.

Serve with mashed potatoes.

Vannes-Style
Tripe

Serves 8.
Preparation: 30 minutes.
Cooking: 5 hours minimum.

1 kg psalterium (3rd stomach) cut into strips,
1 kg rennet stomach (4th stomach) cut into strips,
1 calf's foot cut into four

(ask your butcher to do this),
4 thinly-sliced onions,
2 cloves garlic (chopped),
3 thinly-sliced leeks (white part only),
4 thinly-sliced carrots,
1 bouquet garni (thyme, bay, parsley, celery),
1 dsp. tomato puree,
1 heaped dsp. mustard,
1 beef stock cube,
1 bottle dry sparkling cider,
5 cl cider brandy,
50 g salted butter,
salt, pepper

Heat the butter in a large ovenproof casserole over a medium heat and fry the onions and garlic until golden.

Lay the pieces of calf's foot on the onions. Add the vegetables, then the tripe and the bouquet garni.

Pour in the cider and cider brandy. Season with salt and pepper.

Dissolve the stock cube on the gas or electric ring in 20 cl water.

Add the tomato puree and mustard.

Mix and pour into the tripe.

Cover and bring to boil over a high heat.

Place the casserole in the oven preheated to Th. 5 or 170 ° C and bake for at least 5 hours.

Serve in the casserole.

Garnish with boiled potatoes.

Chicken in Fouesnant Cider.

Duckling in **Shrimp Sauce**

Serves 6.
Preparation: 30 minutes.
Cooking: 55 minutes.

2 small Muscovy ducks, livers and gizzards from ducks,
1 kg cooked, shelled scampi (set aside 6 large scampi for decoration - do not cook),
2 dsp. juniper berries,
1 small pot shrimp paste,
10 cl gin,
3 large dsp. double cream,
1 lemon,
1 heaped dsp. mild paprika,
1 tsp. pink pepper,
1 pinch curry powder,
1 tsp. sugar,
80 g salted butter,
salt, oil

Cross over the claws on the scampi set aside for decoration, lay on a baking sheet, brush with oil, and grill until light golden brown.

Set to one side to decorate the finished dish.

Blend the duck livers and gizzards until creamy with the juniper berries, gin, pink pepper and 1 tsp. salt.

Pour the mixture into the duckling, ensuring that it coats all parts of the interior.

Rub the skin of duckling with half a lemon. Leave until dry. Squeeze the juice remaining in the lemon and blend with the shrimp paste, paprika, curry powder, sugar and a little salt.

Lay the ducklings on a large roasting dish (preferably earthenware). Brush with the shrimp paste mixture, dot each duckling with 40 g butter.

Roast for 40 minutes in the oven preheated to 200 ° C (Th. 6), basting occasionally.

Prick the duckling with the tip of a knife blade. Juices should run clear, with a very slight pink tinge.

Add the fresh cream and shelled scampi. Scrape the base of roasting tray with a spatula (if there is insufficient sauce, add a little water). Baste the duckling again and roast for a further 15 minutes at an oven temperature of 160 ° C (Th. 4).

To serve

Carve the duckling on the serving dish. Pour the scampi sauce over the top. Decorate the edge of the dish with grilled scampi. Serve with carrot puree or creole rice.

Onion **Johnnies'** Veal

Serves 6.
Preparation: 15 mins. Cooking: 1 hr.

1.4 kg sliced leg of veal (with bone in centre), suet from 1 calves kidney,

Lay veal in a large roasting dish, preferably earthenware. Sprinkle with salt, pepper and a good pinch nutmeg.

Lay suet over top and pour on oil.

Cook towards the top of the preheated oven (240° C) so that the meat is well browned. Brown for 20 mins then turn meat, move shelf down to middle of oven, lower temperature to 210° C. Pour shallots around meat, sprinkle with sugar, salt and pepper.

Continue cooking for 40 mins. stirring shallots from time

Canettes « Dames de nage »

4 dsp. oil,
1 kg to **1.2 kg** peeled
shallots (fresh
or frozen),
1 level dsp. sugar,

1 pinch grated
nutmeg,
salt, pepper

to time and basting meat with fat in roasting tray. Do not add water – the shallots should glaze and soften in their own juices.
Serve with mashed potato.

Fricassee

of Wild
Rabbit

Serves 4.
Preparation: 20 minutes.
Cooking: 45 minutes.

1 wild rabbit
(approx. **1.5 kg**) cut
into pieces,
200 g diced smoked
bacon,

20 small shallots
(peeled),
250 g wild
mushrooms
(penny buns, girolles,
craterellus etc.),
1 dsp. plain flour,
20 cl good Muscadet,
1 clove garlic
(crushed),
1 small tsp. savory,
1 bay leaf,
1 sprig thyme,
50 g butter,
2 dsp. oil,
salt, pepper

Blanch the bacon for 5 minutes in boiling water. Drain.
Heat the butter and oil in a stew pan over a medium heat and fry the bacon until transparent. Add the shallots and cook until golden brown, stirring occasionally. Remove the shallots and bacon but leave the fat in the pan.
Brown the pieces of rabbit in the bacon fat, turning over to cook on all sides. When the rabbit is golden, sprinkle with the flour and stir for 1 to 2 minutes before pouring in the white wine and 1/2 glass water. Scrape the bottom of the stew pan with a wooden spatula to ensure that none of the flavour is lost. Add the crushed garlic, savory, thyme, bay leaf, salt and pepper. Bring to the boil then cover and simmer for 15 minutes over a low heat.
Clean the mushrooms, half or quarter, and add to the stew pan with the bacon and shallots. Stir and simmer for further 30 minutes
Serve with saute or mashed potatoes.
This rabbit dish can be made on the previous day and reheated when required.

Fricassee of Wild Rabbit.

Breton-Style Roast Pork.

Breton-Style
Roast Pork

Serves 4.
Preparation: 20 minutes.
Cooking: 1 hr 15 minutes.

*1 kg pork on bone
(loin or shoulder),
3 dsp. mustard,
3 dsp. oil,
6 large cloves garlic,
1 kg potatoes,
150 g salted butter,
salt, pepper*

Preheat the oven to 240 ° C (Th. 8). Peel one clove of garlic and rub it on the meat bone.

Brush the entire joint with mustard. Lay in a large earthenware roasting tray. Season with salt and pepper, brush with oil, and lay the unpeeled cloves of garlic round the edge.

Dot with the butter and roast for 15 minutes. Peel the potatoes, leaving whole if small.

Dry in a cloth and lay out around the meat.

Lower the heat of the oven to 200 ° C (Th. 6) and roast for 1 hr, basting occasionally with the juices from the meat.

Turn the meat once during roasting time.

Kig ha farz Gwiniz du (Pork and Dumpling).

Kig ha farz
Gwiniz du
(Pork and Dumpling)

Serves 8.
Preparation: 1 hour.
Cooking: 2 hr 30.

500 g half-salted bacon,
1 half-salted knuckle of pork,
1 kg chuck steak,
4 smoked sausages,
4 leeks tied together,
1 green cabbage,
8 small carrots (peeled),
4 white turnips (peeled),
1 onion stuck with two cloves,
3 cloves garlic (unpeeled),
1 bouquet garni (thyme, bay leaf, parsley, celery),
sea salt, pepper

For the farz Gwiniz du (dumpling)
500 g buckwheat flour,
4 eggs,
1/2 dsp. sea salt,
20 cl fresh cream,
1 l milk,
100 g melted butter,
1 handful sultanas,
1 canvas bag or teatowel stitched into bag shape,
cooking string

Preparing the stew

Soak the half-salted meats for 3 hours in a large bowl of cold water to remove the brine.

Place the chuck steak, onion, garlic and bouquet garni in a large pan of cold water (4 litres) and bring to the boil over a high heat. Skim and lower the heat.

Add several good pinches of pepper and 1 dsp. sea salt.

Simmer for 30 minutes. Add the half-salted meats and vegetables.

Bring back to the boil over a high heat then lower the heat and simmer for 30 minutes. Add the smoked sausages.

While the meat is cooking, prepare the stuffing

Lightly beat the eggs in a bowl with the fresh cream and sea salt.

Pour the buckwheat flour into a large mixing bowl, make a well in the centre, and pour in the egg and cream mixture. Continue stirring with a wooden spoon and slowly add the milk, melted butter and sultanas.

Leave the dumpling to stand for 30 minutes to 1 hour.

Then place the dumpling in the bag (being careful not to overfill. The dumpling will swell during cooking).

Tie the neck of the bag with string.

Lay a large wooden spoon (or stick) across the pan and attach the bag of stuffing to it so that the bag is suspended in the stew (add more water if necessary).

Stew for 1 1/2 hours.

To serve

Heat soup plates.

Remove the dumpling from the bag and cut into thick slices on the serving dish.

Slice the meat and sausages on another dish and pour over a ladleful of stock. Serve the vegetables in a vegetable dish.

Pour the stock into a small soup tureen.

Guests should serve themselves with meat, vegetables, and slices of dumpling and pour a small ladleful of stock over the top.

If you dampen the bag before placing the dumpling mixture inside, it is easier to remove the dumpling when cooked.

Pheasant
with
Chanterelle
Mushrooms

Serves 4.
Preparation: 20 mins.
Cooking: 1 hr.

1 plump, non-larded pheasant,
3 poultry livers
+ pheasant liver,
4 shallots (chopped),
1/2 clove garlic (crushed),
1 medium glass (15 cl) port,
500 g chanterelle mushrooms (cleaned),
2 heaped dsp. crème fraîche,
80 g softened butter,
salt, pepper,
paprika, oil

Chop poultry and pheasant livers with a generous handful of chanterelle mushrooms.

Add 40 g softened butter, salt, pepper and a pinch of paprika. Stuff pheasant with this mixture then mix crushed garlic with remainder of butter, salt and pepper. Spread butter mixture all over skin of pheasant.

Heat 2 dsp. oil in a pan over medium heat. Gently brown pheasant on all sides for 5 to 6 mins. Add shallots.

Brown lightly for a few minutes. Cover and simmer for 30 mins. over a gentle heat then add chanterelle mushrooms and pour in port. Cover and continue cooking for a further 30 mins.

Remove pheasant from pan. Carve on a serving dish and keep warm. Add cream, a generous pinch of paprika, salt and pepper to the pan.

Stir for 1 min. over heat then pour round pheasant.

Breton
Pork
Stew

Serves 8.
Preparation: 15 mins.
Cooking: 1 hr to 1 1/2 hrs.

1 lightly salted pork knuckle (approx. 1.5 kg),
1 kg lightly-salted belly of pork,
500 g (or more) smoked belly of pork,
8 medium-sized carrots (peeled),
8 leeks (white part only, tied in a bunch),
1 large Savoy cabbage or curly kale (quartered),
8 firm potatoes (peeled),
1 small bouquet garni (thyme, bay, parsley, celery),
salt, pepper corns

Choose good pink meat (a rich colour shows that it has been only lightly salted).

Place in a basin of cold water for 1 hr under a running trickle of water.

Then place knuckle in a large pan with bouquet garni and 1 tsp. pepper corms. Cover with 3 to 4 litres water and bring to boil over a high heat.

Add lightly-salted belly of pork, smoked belly of pork and carrots. Lower heat to medium position and simmer for 30 mins. Skim, add remainder of vegetables and continue cooking for 30 to 40 mins. after stew has returned to the boil.

The meat should remain slightly firm so that it can be sliced.

Slice meat, lay out on serving dish and surround by some of the vegetables.

Serve remainder of vegetables in another serving dish.

Serve with sea salt, mustard and gherkins.

Aven Veal
with Shrimp
coulis

Serves 6.
Preparation: 30 mins.
Cooking: 30 mins.

6 large, thin slices
of veal,
1 tin artichoke hearts
(or artichoke puree),
2 dsp. thick crème
fraîche,
2 dsp. flour (40 g),
50 g butter,
50 g grated parmesan,
12 peeled shrimps,
salt, pepper, butter

Coating:
1 tsp. mustard,
1 tsp. oil,
2 egg yolks,

approx. 6 heaped dsp.
breadcrumbs

Shrimp Coulis:
2 small jars shrimp
butter,
2 dsp. artichoke puree,
1 tsp. tomato puree,
1/2 tsp. curry,
2 dsp. port,
2 dsp. cognac,
3 generous dsp. crème
fraîche

Decoration:
6 slices lemon,
6 tsp. chopped
parsley

Drain artichoke hearts and puree in a blender. Set aside 2 heaped dsp. for shrimp coulis.

Mix remainder with crème fraîche and parmesan.

Melt butter in a small saucepan over a low heat, add flour and cook for 2 or 3 mins. stirring all the time.

Add artichoke puree, salt and pepper and stir until thick and creamy. Remove from heat and set aside to cool.

Spread veal slices on working surface, lay 2 shrimps and 1 spoonful artichoke puree on one half of each slice. Fold other half over filling to form a "pasty".

Close and hold in place using small wooden skewers.

Mix mustard, egg yolks, oil, salt and pepper with a fork in a soup plate. Place breadcrumbs in another soup plate.

Dip veal slices in egg mixture then in breadcrumbs. Lay in an ovenproof dish, overlapping slightly.

Dot with small knobs of butter and cook for 30 mins. at Th. 5 (170° C).

Prepare shrimp coulis: mix all ingredients in a saucepan and heat gently, stirring all the time.

Serve in a sauceboat. Garnish veal slices with lemon and parsley.

Sausage
with Cabbage

Serves 4.
Preparation: 30 minutes.
Cooking: 1 hour.

1 large green cabbage
or kale,
2 sliced onions,
4 carrots (sliced),
8 sausages,
1 heaped dsp. plain
flour,
100 g salted butter,
1 sprig thyme,
1 bay leaf,
salt, pepper

Cut the cabbage in quarters, wash, and remove some of the stalk. Blanch for 3 minutes in a pan of boiling salted water and drain.

Heat half the butter in a pan over a medium heat and brown the sausages. Remove from the pan and set aside on a plate.

Put the onions and carrots in the pan and cook for 3 to 4 minutes till golden. Sprinkle with the flour, add the remainder of the butter and stir to make a light roux paste.

Pour in a glass of water, season with salt and pepper, then add the cabbage, thyme and bay leaf. Cover and turn the heat down low. Simmer for 40 minutes. Stir and lay the sausages on the cabbage.

Cook for a further 20 minutes

Cabbage must be simmered over a very low heat so that it «melts in the mouth» without becoming watery.

Leg of Lamb
Belle-Ile-en-Mer Style

Serves 6 - 8.
Preparation: 15 minutes.
Cooking: 45 minutes.

1 Belle-Ile leg of lamb
(2.5 - 3 kg),
7.5 cl cider brandy,
3 large cloves garlic
(finely crushed),
1 dsp. thyme leaves,
70 g salted butter
(softened),
4 dsp. breadcrumbs,
salt, pepper,
curry powder.

Accompaniment when cooking leg of lamb
3 large heads garlic,
fresh if possible, left
whole and unpeeled,
placed round roast

Accompaniment
1.5 kg fresh white
haricot beans (local
varieties include Breton
cocos and Paimpol
ingots),
1 large onion (roughly
chopped),
2 cloves garlic
(unpeeled),
1 sprig thyme,
1 bay leaf,
1 beef stock cube,
50 g salted butter,
salt, pepper

Cooking the beans
Melt the onion in the butter over a low heat in a thick-bottomed stew pan. Add the beans and cover with water. Season with salt and pepper, add the stock cube, unpeeled garlic, thyme and bay leaf. Cover, bring to boil, then lower the heat and simmer for 45 minutes, stirring occasionally and adding a little water if necessary.

Cooking the leg of lamb
Preheat the oven to maximum heat.
Using a sharp-pointed knife, mark out a grid pattern on the fleshy part of the roast. Lay the meat on an earthenware roasting tray and pour over the cider brandy.
Leave to dry for 5 minutes. Blend the softened butter with the crushed garlic, thyme, a good pinch of curry powder, the breadcrumbs, salt and pepper. Brush this mixture all over the leg of lamb.
Wrap each head of garlic in aluminium foil and lay in the roasting tray around the roast.
Put the roast in the oven, lower the temperature to 200 ° C (Th. 6) after 10 minutes, and roast for a further 35 minutes basting occasionally.

To serve
Crush the heads of garlic in a vegetable mill or with a fork. Mix the garlic puree into the defatted sauce and serve in a sauce boat.
Serve with beans and mashed potatoes (if liked).

Grandmother's Potted Pork

Serves 6 to 8.
Preparation: 5 mins.
Cooking: 3 hrs. 20 mins.

1 kg spare rib
with bones (not too lean
and chopped into
pieces),

1 piece fatty fresh
bacon rind,
1 glass (20 cl)
Muscadet,
1.5 glasses (30 cl)
water,
1 dsp. cider brandy
or Calvados,
1 small sprig thyme,
1 bay leaf,
3 large cloves garlic
(not peeled),
salt, pepper

Line base of a casserole (preferably cast iron) with rind then add meat, salt and pepper. Top with thyme, bay leaf and garlic.
Pour in wine, water and cider brandy.
Cover and cook for 3 hrs. over a very low heat.
Remove thyme, bay leaf, garlic and bones.
Mash meat with a fork while still in casserole.
Return to a low heat for a further 20 mins, stirring occasionally.
Taste, check seasoning, pour into terrine, leave to cool then place in the fridge.
It can be kept for 8 days.

Leg of Lamb Belle-Ile-en-Mer Style.

Savoury Buckwheat Pancakes

Makes approx. 20 pancakes.
Preparation : 20 minutes
plus «standing» time
(several hours or even
overnight).

500 g buckwheat
flour,
4 dsp. wheat flour
(approx. 70 g),
1 egg,
1 tsp. salt,
1 jug cold water,
3 dsp. oil,
1 cup milk.

To cook pancakes
1 cup softened butter
(for griddle),
250 g salted butter
placed beside griddle
to butter pancakes,
1 cast-iron griddle or
1 non-stick
flat-rimmed frying
pan,
1 wad of fabric rolled
up and tied
with string to grease
the griddle,
1 palette knife or thin
wooden spatula.
The batter can also be
spread out using
a scraper but
I would advise
against this as it
requires a certain
degree of dexterity.

Making the Batter

Pour the flour into a large mixing bowl, and make a well in centre. Add the salt to the well and break the egg into it. Mix the batter with a wooden spoon, beginning with the egg and gradually working in the flour. At same time, slowly pour in the cold water, still pouring into the centre.

When the batter has the same consistency as thick mayonnaise, beat for 10 minutes with a hand whisk or use an electric mixer on a low speed. The more the batter is beaten, the lighter it is and the easier it is to spread on the griddle.

Add more water, blending in with a soup ladle. The batter must be absolutely smooth and run off the ladle like cream (N.B. be careful not to add too much water).

Cover the bowl with a cloth and leave for few hours, or over-night, in a cool place.

Just before making the pancakes, stir again with the ladle, adding the oil and a small quantity of milk until the batter runs smoothly again but still coats the ladle.

Cooking the pancakes

Grease the griddle with the wad of fabric dipped in softe-ned butter. Place the griddle over the heat and, when it is very hot and the butter is beginning to smoke, pour on a small lad-leful of batter (it is better to pour slightly too much than too little).

Spread the batter by tilting the griddle in all directions and tip any excess batter back into the bowl, holding the griddle almost upright to do so.

Cook the pancake for 2 minutes, or until the centre is no lon-ger liquid. To turn the pancake over, grasp the edge between your thumb and forefinger, lay it over the palette knife then quickly lift it and flip over. Immediately dot the other side with a generous knob of salted butter.

Leave to cook for few seconds, fold the pancake in four and serve immediately.

If you want to make pancakes in advance and fill them later, do not butter the second side and spread the pancakes out on a dry tea towel as you make them.

Reheating the pancakes

Grease and heat the griddle over a medium-high heat.
Lay the pancake on the griddle, heat for 1 minute, then turn over, and add a knob of butter or a filling.

There are hundreds of fillings for pancakes.

The few suggestions below were chosen because the method of preparation seemed to me to be important.

Savoury Buckwheat Pancakes.

PANCAKE WITH EGG

Heat the pancake, turn over, add butter, pour an egg yolk onto the centre of the pancake, season with salt and pepper.

Immediately fold the edges in towards the centre, leaving the egg uncovered (the pancake forms a rectangle). Slip onto a plate and serve.

PANCAKE WITH TRIPLE FILLING

Proceed as above but lay a thin slice of ham between the pancake and the egg then sprinkle grated Swiss cheese on top. Fold the pancake in half.

PANCAKE WITH BRETON SAUSAGE

Pour 1/4 in. water in a frying pan, add sausages. Cover and cook over a low heat until the water has been absorbed. Remove the lid, turn up the heat, and cook the sausages until golden brown, shaking the frying pan occasionally. Split the sausages lengthways and fill the pancakes.

Serve pancakes with cider, buttermilk or curds.

Sweet Pancakes

Equipment

1 mixing bowl,
1 long-handled wooden spoon,
1 soup ladle,
1 palette knife or wooden slice,
2 griddles or non-stick pancake pans with low rims,
1 wad of fabric or kitchen paper for greasing the pan.

Lower Brittany Pancake Batter

Makes approximately 24 pancakes.
Preparation: 10 minutes + 1 hour to «stand»

250 g white flour,
3 dsp. buckwheat flour,
1 egg,
120 g sugar,
120 g salted butter (melted),
25 cl full-cream milk,
25 cl water,
1 tsp. cinnamon,
1 tsp. orange flower water,
2 dsp. cider brandy or Calvados (apple brandy),
150 g (approx.) softened butter to grease griddle

Mix the two types of flour together in a bowl. Make a well in the centre and break in the egg. Add the sugar. Begin to mix the batter from the centre outwards with the wooden spoon, gradually adding the water then the milk.

Mix slowly until the batter is smooth.

Add the melted butter, cinnamon, orange flower water and brandy. Mix again then leave to stand for 1 hour.

Cooking the pancakes

Lightly grease two pancake pans. Put the first griddle over a high heat; the second one over a low heat.

Give the batter a final stir with the soup ladle, then pour a small ladleful of batter onto the first griddle, over a high heat, as soon as the pan is very hot. Tilt the griddle in all directions to ensure that the batter covers the entire base of the pan, then pour any excess off into the mixing bowl.

Cook over a high heat until the centre of pancake is no longer liquid. Grasp the edge of pancake between the thumb and forefinger of your left hand, lay it over a slice or palette knife then quickly lift and flip over onto the second griddle. Leave to cook while you prepare the next pancake on the first pan, greasing it before you pour on the batter.

Serve the cooked pancake as it is, or with butter, or with a filling.

If you want to make pancakes half-an-hour or an hour in advance, keep them warm on a plate covered with aluminium foil, over a saucepan of simmering water.

If you want to make pancakes several hours in advance and reheat them as required, spread them out on a dry tea towel to cool. They can then be piled up, wrapped in aluminium foil, and stored in a cool place for 24 hours.

Reheating pancakes

Butter the griddle(s) again and heat the pancake for 30 seconds on each side.

To reheat vacuum-packed shop pancakes, which are drier than home-made pancakes, dampen slightly with a brush dipped in cold milk just before placing on the griddle.

PANCAKES WITH SWEET CIDER

Make in the same way as Lower Brittany Pancakes but replace the water and milk with 50 cl of sweet cider (this is the first juice extracted from apples being pressed for cider-making).

Prune-filled Batter Pudding.

Prune-filled
Batter
Pudding

Serves 6.
Preparation: 10 minutes.
Cooking: 40 mins.

250 g (approx.) prunes,
125 g flour,
125 g sugar,
2 sachets
vanilla-flavoured sugar,
4 eggs,
3 dsp. rum,
1 tsp. baking powder,
3/4 l. full-cream milk,
1 pinch salt,
butter for cake tin

Preheat the oven to 240 ° C (Th. 8).

Pour the flour into a mixing bowl, and mix in the sugar, vanilla-flavoured sugar, salt and baking powder. Make a well in the centre. Break the eggs into the well then mix with a wooden spoon, beginning at the centre and gradually working in the flour.

Heat the milk with the rum and prunes. Slowly pour the milk onto the batter, stirring vigorously and keeping back the prunes until last.

Pour into the greased cake tin and place in the oven.

Bake for 10 minutes at 240 ° C then turn the oven down to 200 ° C (Th. 6) and bake for a further 30 minutes. Leave to cool slightly before removing from the tin.

29

Breton Cake

Ø 26 cm (10 in.) sponge tin.
Preparation: 15 minutes.
Cooking: 45 minutes.

350 g flour,
1 egg and
5 egg yolks,
300 g sugar,
1 sachet vanilla-flavoured sugar,
350 g well-softened salted butter,
1 dsp. orange flower water

Glaze:
1 egg yolk mixed with
1 tsp. milk and
1/2 tsp. sugar.
Butter for cake tin

Pour the flour into a large mixing bowl and mix in the sugar and vanilla-flavoured sugar. Make a well in the centre. Break in the eggs, softened butter, and orange flower water.

Stir with a wooden spoon until all the ingredients are mixed in then work into a ball.

Generously grease the sponge tin.

Preheat the oven to 180 ° C (Th. 5 or 6). Place the dough in the tin then flatten out.

Brush with the egg yolk mixture and drag a fork across the surface to mark out a grid pattern.

Bake for 45 to 50 minutes in the oven. The cake should be pale golden in colour and very springy to the touch.

Leave to cool before removing from the tin.

Fanch's Kouign-Amann

(Breton «Lardy Cake»)

Serves 6 to 8.
Preparation: 15 minutes.
Rising time: 1 hour.
Cooking: 20 minutes.

300 g flour,
15 g fresh baker's yeast,
18 cl warm water
(1 dsp. water = 2 cl),
250 g good-quality salted butter (softened),
250 g sugar,
1 level tsp. salt

Stir the yeast into the warm water and leave to rise for 10 minutes then pour onto the flour in the mixing bowl and add salt.

Mix and beat the dough by hand for 5 to 10 minutes.

Cover the bowl with a cloth and leave the dough to rise for 1 hour in a warm place until it has doubled in size.

Preheat the oven to 220 ° C (Th. 7).

Dust the working surface with flour and flatten the dough by hand until it is approx. 1 in. thick. Place 200 g butter and 200 g sugar in the centre of the dough and fold the edges over the top, enclosing the ingredients.

Place the cake in a cake tin (preferably ovenproof porcelain) and again fold over the edges of the dough, pressing your fist into the centre to make a small dip in the centre of the cake.

Soften 50 g butter until almost melted and drip over the dough. Sprinkle with 50 g sugar and place in oven.

Put an oven tray filled with water on the shelf underneath and bake for 20 minutes.

The water in the oven will create a humid heat, making the Kouign-Amann deliciously soft.

You can also make a Kouign-Amann with commercial ready-to-use bread dough.

Breton cake.

Ya-Ya's
Apple Cake

Serves 6 to 8.
Preparation: 20 mins.
Cooking: 30 mins.

*500 g sharp
juicy apples
(Bramleys),*

*3 glasses (60 cl)
warm full-cream milk,
2 glasses sugar,
2 glasses flour,
2 large eggs,
180 g well softened
salted butter,
1 sachet raising agent,
1/2 tsp. salt,
1 sachet vanilla sugar*

Mix sugar, salt and eggs in a bowl.

Stir with wooden spoon and gradually blend in sieved flour and raising agent.

End with well-softened (almost melted) butter and warm milk.

Peel and roughly slice apples. Add to mixture.

Grease a non-stick sponge tin with butter and pour in cake mixture.

Bake for 30 mins. in a preheated oven (Th. 6 or 200° C).

Remove from oven and immediately sprinkle with vanilla sugar. Leave to cool slightly before removing from tin.

Best eaten warm.

Table of Contents

Fabric kindly supplied by the Etablissements François Le Villec in Quimper. All rights reserved.

© 2001 Edilarge S.A. Editions Ouest-France , Rennes.
Imprimé en France par Calligraphy Print, Rennes (35)
ISBN 2.7373.2234.0 - N° d'éditeur : 3622.03.1,5.01.05
Dépôt légal : Mars 2001 - N° d'imprimeur 17181